D1521327

The CALCULATING Book

FUN & GAMES
with your
POCKET CALCULATOR

The CALCULATING Book

FUN & GAMES with your POCKET CALCULATOR

James T. Rogers

Illustrations by Bob Korn

Random House New York

Library of Congress Cataloging in Publication Data
Rogers, James T
  The calculating book.
    1. Calculating-machines—Problems, exercises, etc. 2.
Mathematical recreations. I. Title.
QA75.R62   793.7'4   74-29606
ISBN 0-394-73033-X

Manufactured in the United States of America
9 8 7 6 5 4 3

To Martin Gardner
Colleague, counselor and friend

One evening I was sitting in the rooms of the Analytical Society at Cambridge, my head leaning forward on the Table in a kind of dreamy mood, with a Table of logarithms lying open before me. Another member coming into the room, and seeing me half asleep, called out, "Well, Babbage, what are you dreaming about?" to which I replied, "I am thinking that all these Tables [pointing to the logarithms] might be calculated by machinery."

Charles Babbage
Passages from the Life of a Philosopher (1864)

The

CALCULATING
Book

FUN & GAMES
with your
POCKET CALCULATOR

Say 107734

All right. You have laid hold of a pocket calculator, the electronic whiz kid of the seventies, and you have mastered the art of balancing your checkbook and checking the checker at the supermarket by adding up the cost of the things you have loaded into your shopping cart. (It is an art because of the calculator's trait of keeping to itself, after one dutiful display of each, the entries you have made during a calculation. Lacking a printout, you have to be careful about not skipping a figure or repeating one). This book aims to show you a great many more things you can do with your calculator.

One of them is that you can make the machine talk, provided that you are willing to settle for words that contain the letters *e, h, i, l, o* and *s*. Try 107734, entering the numbers and then turning the calculator 180 degrees so that you are reading the display upside down.

A trickier way of having the machine show off its vocabulary is to think of the word you want and then work up a problem that will give you the word. During the gasoline crunch of 1974, for example, a funny that was making the rounds of calculator freaks was, Where did you get gas today? Multiply 142.15469 by 5 and read the

[3]

answer upside down. Another response to the same question can be obtained by multiplying 284.02212 by 2.5 and reading the answer upside down.

In assembling this book I have made two assumptions about you as a reader. The first is that you are not a mathematical wizard. (The calculator is, of course, but it is just as proficient at $2+2$ as it is at $573.881 \div 72.77$.) The second is that you are fairly innocent about pocket calculators.

It would probably be helpful if I could dilate a little on how to operate a calculator. The trouble is that one make of calculator is unlikely to operate in exactly the same way as another. The best thing for you to do is read the operating instructions that come with your machine and then play around with the thing for a while. You will find that your proficiency increases rapidly.

A few points are basic to the operation of any machine. Beware of lost or repeated numbers; as I have mentioned, the machine won't give you a cumulative written record of the numbers you have entered during a calculation. You have to be your own memory bank, and the best way (when you are dealing with anything more complicated than a couple of numbers) is to keep a pencil and a piece of paper at hand and jot down the numbers that you think you may need a record of.

It is also helpful to bear in mind the difference between a "chain" operation and an operation involving a "constant" if you have the kind of calculator that offers you a choice. A chain operation is what you are likely to want most of the time. The chain can be as simple as $2+2$ or as complicated as $591 \times 58.27 + 93 \div 11 - 3281$. The calculator can carry on like this indefinitely but will yield its result as soon as you press the $=$ key.

A constant feature, if your calculator has one, is for the relatively infrequent occasions when you want to use the same number in a lot of calculations. If you want to multiply a series of numbers by 15, for example, the constant feature (however it works on your make of calculator) will make the business easier. When you have a machine with a switch that gives you a choice between "chain" and "constant," however, be careful not to leave it on constant after you have finished the calculation involving a constant number. Otherwise you may get some crazy answers on subsequent chain calculations.

You also need to be mindful of the consequences of hitting the key that clears the calculator. When you do it, you erase everything that's in the machine. Frequently that's just what you want to do, but if you're in the middle of a calculation and you press the clear key by error, you will have to start the calculation over again at the beginning.

(Some calculators have an additional key that will let you clear only the number that you just entered, so that if you are, say, adding a long column of figures and you make a mistake in entering one, you can erase that number alone and put in the correct one.)

Your calculator probably has an eight-digit display. That's more than adequate for most purposes, but it can be a limitation if you want to multiply big numbers (such as 2,515,826 by 7,612,015) or to have an answer that is accurate to more decimal places than the calculator can provide.

Which brings me to the floating decimal point. A calculator with this feature automatically puts the decimal point where it belongs, but when it comes to the end of its display space, it stops, lopping off the numbers that otherwise would appear to the right of the decimal point. This is seldom likely to be a hindrance to you, but if you wanted to multiply something like 55,612.31 by 58.412 and wanted to know the answer to more than one decimal place, you would be out of luck, because with that calculation the machine would run out of display space after 3248426.2. Back to the pencil-and-paper method you go.

A low-priced calculator may not have the floating-decimal feature. It will probably give you two digits to the right of the decimal point, but no more. Such a machine will do right by you on $156.73 − $49.18, but it cannot cope properly with 156.73 × 49.18. A calculator with a floating decimal point will line out 7707.9814 without so much as a stammer.

You also want to be on the lookout for signs that the battery in your calculator is running down, which can happen quickly if you leave the machine on too long. A typical sign is that the numbers on the display don't light up properly. It's a good rule of thumb to turn the calculator off whenever as much as a minute is likely to pass before you start your next calculation.

The tricks, games and maneuvers in this book have all been worked out on a standard, medium-priced calculator that does only arithmetical things: +, −, × and ÷. It is not the fancy kind with keys such as $\sqrt{}$, y^x, % and *cos*. It does, however, have a floating-decimal feature and a chain-constant switch, although for most of the things in the book the lack of either of those features won't matter.

The pocket calculator is the ideal instrument for the person who is all thumbs, either in the usual sense or mathematically. In fact, the fastest way to operate one of these machines is to cradle it in the fingers of your two hands and flail away at the keys with your thumbs. The crucial point

is this: Do not be daunted by the thing. You are its Aladdin, and it is your genie.

Thumbs bring me to a final point. I started this book with the intention of organizing the games and tricks into groups whose components would have a cousinly relationship. But as I went along I came gradually to what might be called the Little Jack Horner Principle: you put in your thumb and pull out a plum. To that end I have for the most part simply tossed the ingredients into the pie. (The major exception is the Nutcracker Suite at the end of the book, where you will find a group of things that are either mathematically a little deeper than the earlier ones or require somewhat more proficiency with the calculator.) Therefore it doesn't much matter where you dip into the book. I only hope that you will regard whatever you pull out as a plum.

J.T.R.

A few extraordinarily rich men have displayed the quirk of never carrying any cash. One of them was seized with a desire for a soft drink as he went past a soft-drink machine on a hot afternoon; as usual, he had to turn to an aide for the cash, which in those memorable days was a dime.

People like that couldn't work this trick without turning to the aide or pretending to have some change. Presumably you aren't in that predicament. If you just happen to be without any change, however, you can pretend too.

Enter on the calculator (making sure that it is in the chain mode) a figure that is double your age. Add 5 and multiply by 50. Add the amount of change that you have in your pocket, up to one dollar, but enter it as a whole number rather than a decimal number. Subtract the number of days in a year (365), add 115 and divide by 100. Now, at last, you can push the = key and see what has been going on in there. Your calculator will display one or two numbers to the left of the decimal point (one if you are less than ten years old, two if you are ten or more) and two to the right. The number or numbers on the left will be your age, and the numbers on the right will be the amount of change that you entered in the calculation.

Entertain a friend today. Hand him your calculator and a calendar and ask him to add the dates of any three successive days in a week and the dates of the corresponding days in the following two weeks—nine numbers in all. (The days should all be in the same month.) Now he clears the calculator and hands it to you, remembering what the total of the nine numbers was.

Ask him for the first date and enter it on the calculator. Add 8 to it and multiply the result by 9. Your total will be the same as his. (If nobody is around to be dazzled by this trick, you can always work it yourself.)

Here is another game of singles or doubles involving a calendar. Taking a calendar page for any month, your victim draws (or you do it if you have no victim) a boundary around the sixteen days represented by any four days of the first week and the corresponding days of the next three weeks. Add mentally or on the calculator any pair of dates in diagonally opposite corners. Double the result and make a note of the answer.

Now circle any one of the sixteen dates within the boundary on the calendar page and cross out the horizontal and vertical rows in which the circled date appears. Repeat the process with two more dates that have not been crossed out. By then only one date will remain that is neither circled nor crossed out.

With the calculator add the three circled dates and the one that was neither circled nor crossed out. The result will be the number that you made note of before you started all that circling and crossing out.

Enter on the calculator the year of your birth. Add to that number the year when something else important took place in your life. To the sum that you have add your age and the number of years that have passed since the second Important Event. (Figure these numbers to the present year. If you were born in October 1940, for example, and it is now July of 1975, your age is in fact thirty-four but as of 1975 it is thirty-five. Use 35.) Divide by 2, push the = key and observe the display. (If it doesn't show the present year, you have done something wrong.)

$$- \overset{\square}{\underset{\times}{\overset{=}{\underset{\div}{+}}}} -$$

Mumbo jumbo. Enter a number, double it, add another number, halve the result and subtract the original number. The calculator will display a number that is half the number you added after doubling the original number.

With the calculator in the chain mode, you can do all this without pushing the = key until the end. An example would be: $653 \times 2 + 953 \div 2 - 653 = 476.5$.

$$- \overset{\square}{\underset{\times}{\overset{=}{\underset{\div}{+}}}} -$$

Punch into the machine any three-digit number with first and last digits that are not the same. Subtract the number that you obtain by reversing the three digits ($463 - 364$, for example, or $387 - 783$). Do this with several numbers and note that in all the answers the middle digit as well as the sum of the first and last digits is always 9. For example, $463 - 364 = (0)99$, and $387 - 783 = -396$.

Now add the answer you get to its reverse, treating negative numbers as positive. (In the example above you would clear the machine and then add 396 and 693, ignoring the fact that 396 was negative when it first popped out of the calculator.) The result will always be 1089.

One of the endearing things about 9 is that it is forever lurking around and likely to jump out at you from unexpected places. For example, if you pick any number (say 4837) and mix its digits (say 7834) and then subtract the smaller number from the larger one (7834−4837), the digits of the result (2997 in this case) will always add to 9 or to a multiple of 9. If you keep adding the digits of successive results (2+7 here, since 2+9+9+7=27), you will ultimately end with a single 9.

The late Royal Vale Heath decorated this principle with some hocus-pocus to present a trick in which your telephone number was transformed into your age. The trick began with the last four digits of the telephone number, although in these days of all-digit numbers, when pleasant exchange names such as MUrray Hill and BUtterfield have been forced to the sidelines, you could work the trick with the whole telephone number. You duly mixed the four digits, subtracted the smaller number from the larger one and added the digits of successive results until you were left with a single digit, which would of course be 9, although Heath did not call attention to that. You added 7 to the single digit, then added the last two digits of the year of your birth and then subtracted 16. The answer is the last two digits of the year of your birth, and by subtracting them from the last two digits of the current year you arrive inevitably at your age as of this year's birthday. If you were born in 1938, for example, the calculation would be: $9+7+38-16=38$, which you would subtract from the last two digits of the current year.

Pick any three digits from 1 through 9 and write them down as a three-digit number. Let's call them a, b and c. (For example, if the number is 238, 2 is a, 3 is b and 8 is c.) Now run through the following chain on the calculator: $a \times 2 + 3 \times 5 + b \times 10 + c - 150$. The answer will be the three-digit number you wrote down.

For this trick you need to be at least ten years old. The age requirement isn't because of the sophistication of the trick—any eight-year-old could do it— but because of the arithmetic.

To your present age (as of this year's birthday) add your age next year. Multiply the result by 5. Add the last digit of the year of your birth. Subtract 5. The result will be a three-digit number. The first two digits of it will be your age, and the third will be the last digit of the year you were born.

If you are under ten and insist on doing the trick, you will get a two-digit answer. The first digit will be your age and the second will be the final digit of the year of your birth.

Your calculator is well schooled in American history. The calculation 32159×464 will cause the machine to give you two important dates in the development of America. Moreover, 33928.75×12 will give you the name of a famous Civil War battle if you read the result upside down.

Haul out of your well-stocked mind a number between 1 and 50. Make a note of it. For the moment let's call it *a*. Pick another number between 50 and 100 and make a note of it. We'll call it b. Now, on the calculator, subtract a from 99 and add b to the result. The answer will be a three-digit number, such as 139. In your head (you don't need a calculator for this) remove the first digit (1) and add it to the other two ($39+1=40$). Subtract the result from b and your answer will be a.

Suppose a is 44 and b is 73. Then $99-44+73=128$; adding the 1 to the 28 gives you 29, and $73-29=44$.

If these numbers strike you as trifling, you can work the trick with bigger numbers. Make a a number between 100 and 200 and b a number between 200 and 1000. Subtract a from 999 and add b to the result. You will wind up with a four-digit number such as 1553. Add 1 to 553 and subtract the result (554) from b. Your calculator will dutifully display a.

Pick a number. Add to it the next higher number. Add 9, divide by 2 and subtract the original number. The answer will be 5. Always.

This is too cheap a shot to allow any mystery to be associated with it. If you write the problem down as $x+(x+1)+9÷2-x=5$ and then cancel the x's, you will see that all you have done (notwithstanding the fandango about x) is add 1 to 9 and divide by 2.

[18]

Several of the other tricks in this book are pretty much in the same class, but you should have the pleasure of discovering which ones they are, and so I will say nothing more about what is going on under the green baize.

Stuck needle. Using 37 as a constant divider and dividing it into anything except an even multiple of 37, you will find that the pattern of numbers to the right of the decimal point invariably repeats itself in groups of three.

You can't do this one, of course, if your calculator doesn't have a floating decimal point, but the lack of a constant feature won't matter. Just do a series of separate divisions: $81 \div 37$, $953 \div 37$ and so on. If your calculator has an eight-digit display, as most of them do, the trick will work only if you divide 37 into numbers less than 3700. Beyond that you are pushing the display past its limit and will get only a small part of the repeating pattern to the right of the decimal point.

You can make your machine develop lockjaw

by going through the steps required to convert degrees Fahrenheit to degrees Celsius (centigrade): F°−32×5÷9=C°. If the answer has a decimal point, as is usually the case, all the numbers to the right of the decimal point (except sometimes the first one) will be the same, such as .2222222.

With a spectator at hand you can employ the calculator to do a bit of showboating. Announce that you are prepared to give the sum of all the odd numbers up to and including whatever odd number the spectator chooses. He will probably assume that you will put the calculator through the plodding exercise of 1+3+5+7 and so on. You may assume that too, but there's a shortcut. Increase the spectator's number by 1. (If he chose 57, start with 58.) Divide by 2 and square the result. You will have the desired total.

The showboating need not be over. Announce that you can just as readily produce the total of all the numbers, both odd and even, up to and including a given odd number.

In this case you proceed as before. Increase the spectator's number by 1, divide by 2 and square the result, taking note this time of the number that you are squaring. Double the answer and subtract the number that you squared. You will have the sum of all the numbers from 1 to the odd number chosen by your collaborator. With 57 as the chosen odd number, the steps would be as follows: $57 + 1 \div 2 = 29$; 29^2 (that is, 29×29) is 841; double 841 is 1682, and $1682 - 29$ (the number you squared) is 1653. That's your answer.

If you rent a car, you are a 335537. (Again, read the display upside down.)

This could be called a recipe for scrambling eggs. Choose any three numbers that are between 10 and 45 and that differ from one another by the same amount; 12, 14 and 16 would do, and so would 14, 28 and 42.

Add the three numbers and write down the result. Multiply the result first by 34. Write down the answer. Clear the machine and multiply your original result by 67. The two answers will be reversed pairs, such as 2856 and 5628, which is what you get when you start with 14, 28 and 42.

In case the world's biggest floating crap game has eluded you, here is a dice game that you can play with yourself. You can also ask somebody else to throw the dice, whereupon you can impress him with the craftiness of the calculator.

Throw a pair of dice. Take the number that shows on the top of either one of them and do the following things: multiply by 2, add 1, multiply by 5, add the number that shows on the top of the second die and subtract 5. The two-digit number that you get as a result will be the two numbers that showed on the dice when you threw them.

Pick any three consecutive numbers from 1 through 49. You'd better write them down, because after you finish running the labyrinth you may lose track of them. Let's say that the numbers are 14, 15 and 16.

Add the numbers, plus a multiple of 3 (say 21) and multiply by 67. The result will be a four-digit number $(14+15+16+21\times67=4422)$.

Now focus on the last two digits of that number (22). Clear the machine and from them subtract the number you get by dividing your multiple of 3 by 3 and adding 1 to the result (in this case $21 \div 3 = 7$ and $7 + 1 = 8$, so you subtract 8 from 22). Your result will be the first of the three original numbers.

If you have inveigled a friend into this, you can readily tell him what his three original numbers were. (In this case you have to get him to do the arithmetic, telling you what multiple of 3 he is using and the last two digits of his four-digit result. Then you perform the necessary operations on that number and announce to him the three numbers he started with. To put a little frosting on the cake, multiply the number formed by the last two digits of his four-digit result by 2, and you will get the first two digits of the four-digit number, whereupon you can tell him what it was.)

The number 37037 yields some intriguing results when you multiply it by the numbers from 3 through 27. Try it with 3 and the multiples of 3 first, and then do it with the nonmultiples of 3.

Now your informative and versatile machine is going to tell you the month and day of your birth, together with your age. Hold on to your hat.

Take the number representing the month of your birth (January is 1, February, 2, and so on) and multiply it by 100. Add the date of your birth. Multiply by 2, add 9, multiply by 5, add 8, multiply by 10, subtract 422, add your age and subtract 108. The result will be a five-digit number; the first digit will tell the month of your birth, the next two the date of your birth (as, say, 08 if it was before the 10th of the month) and the last two your age.

In case you have any doubt about your age, or are of uncertain age, the calculator will drive it home to you and anybody who is watching. The formula is: age×7×1443. Another formula that will be equally relentless on the subject is: age× 3×3367.

Guaranteed result. Take a number. (Write it down.) Add 25 to it and multiply the answer by 2. Subtract 4, divide by 2 and subtract the original number. The answer will always be 23.

Another guaranteed result, this time with big numbers to toss around. Begin with a five-digit number—not quite any number, but one with first and last digits that differ by more than one (43712 would be all right, but 43713 wouldn't). Make a note of it. Now create a new number by reversing the first and last digits of the original number (43712 becomes 23714). Subtract the smaller number from the larger one. Make a note of the answer. Reverse the first and last digits of that number, but now add the two numbers. The answer will always be 109989.

With 43712 as the starting number, you would proceed as follows: $43712 - 23714 = 19998$, and $19998 + 89991 = 109989$.

The trick will also work with starting numbers of four, six and seven digits, producing answers of 10989, 1099989 and 10999989 respectively.

$$-\ \frac{\square}{\begin{array}{c}=\\+\\\div\\\times\end{array}}\ -$$

Here is a fraction-loser, which could also be called 2 much. It involves multiplying any two numbers—say 68 and 43.

Make each one the beginning of a column:

68   43

Now, working with the column on the left, enter a second number, which you obtain by dividing 68 by 2. Proceed down the column, dividing each result by 2 and ignoring fractions, until you reach 1.

The next action involves building up the column on the right by multiplying each result by 2. You will wind up with:

68	43
34	86
17	172
8	344
4	688
2	1376
1	2752

Cross out every even number in the left-hand column and the corresponding number, the number opposite it, in the right-hand column (everything but 17 and 172 and 1 and 2752 in this case). Add the numbers that remain in the

right-hand column (172 + 2752) and you will have
the answer to your multiplication problem (68 ×
43 = 2924).

We have here a street-corner philanthropist
who goes around handing out ten-dollar bills.
(John D. Rockefeller handed out dimes, but you
know about inflation.) The problem is to find how
many ten-dollar bills he started with on a given
day, when his philanthrophy went as follows: To
the first person he met he gave one ten-dollar bill
more than half the number of bills he started with.
To the second he gave two more than half of the
number left after his first gift, and to the third he
gave three more than half of the number left after
his second donation By then he was down to his
last ten-dollar bill. How many did he start with?

A good way to go at this is to take a guess at
the number of bills he started with and then work
it out to see if he has one left at the end. Suppose
you guess that he started with 50. Then to the first
person he would have given half of them plus one,
or 26, and with 26 of his 50 gone he would have
had 24 remaining in his wallet. Then the next
beneficiary would get half of them plus two, or 14,
and the philanthropist would have 10 bills still

in hand. Now comes the third person, who gets half of those plus three, or 8. The philanthropist is left with 2 bills, so your guess was wrong. Try another and go through the same procedure.

In case your calculator (either the machine or the one in your head) stutters over this one, the answer is $x \div 2$, where x is made up of the last two digits in the title of a famous novel by George Orwell.

Our philanthropist started with 42 of the $10 bills.

The number 102564 has an unusual property: you can multiply it by 4 without doing any work, except to shift the 4 from last place to first place. Naturally you'll wind up doing the work anyway in order to check the answer. An alternative is to divide 410256 by 4. Also try $820512 \div 4$.

Give a friend your calculator and ask him to compile a list of ten numbers in which each number is the sum of the preceding two numbers. For example, 7, 10, 17, 27, 44, 71, 115, 186, 301 and 487. (The formal name for a list of numbers obtained in this way is a Fibonacci series.) Have him add the total of the ten numbers but keep the answer to himself.

Now ask to see the list. Tell him that by entering only two numbers on the calculator you will arrive at the answer that he has kept to himself. Take the number that is fourth from last on the list (115 in this case) and multiply it by 11. The answer (1265) will be the same one that he obtained by adding all ten numbers on the list.

If nobody is around to be impressed with your mastery of the Fibonacci series, be your own friend.

You will be involved in another remarkable series if you begin with a number having one or two digits and build up the series by adding the sums of the squares. Suppose you start with 27. You then want to square 2, clear the calculator, square 7, clear again, and then add the two sums (4 and 49) to get the next number in the series. The next number in the series is therefore 53. Now you want to proceed similarly with 5 and 3. The series builds up as follows: 27, 53, 34 [25+9], 25, 29, 85, 89.

Invariably you will wind up with 89 or 1. Starting with 79, for example, you arrive quickly at 1: 79, 130, 10, 1. If you start with a number that gets you to 89 and you continue to build up the series past 89, you will find that it is an unvarying cycle that always returns to 89: 89, 145, 42, 20, 4, 16, 37, 58, 89.

$$- \begin{matrix} \square \\ = \\ + \\ \div \\ \times \end{matrix} -$$

The number 3025 displays a remarkable quirk when it is split into two parts, 30 and 25. Add the two parts and square the result.

$$- \begin{matrix} \square \\ = \\ + \\ \div \\ \times \end{matrix} -$$

No need for you to count sheep any more when you can't sleep. The calculator will do it for you, provided that you have a calculator with a constant feature. Put the calculator on constant, enter 10000000 and make 1.0000001 the constant multiplier. Thereafter the number at the right end of the display will rise by 1 every time you press the = key.

Similarly you can get the machine to count backward by entering 10000000 and making 1.0000001 the constant divider. (Remember, when you finish this puzzle, put the calculator back on chain.)

Your calculator can give you advice on driving. Suppose you are cruising along at 85 miles per hour and you want to know what advice your calculator would offer in that situation. Divide 85 by 79.069767 and read the answer upside down. (If you are driving that fast, maybe it would be better if you put yourself upside down and left the calculator right side up.)

If you want to talk back to the calculator, giving it either an instruction or an opinion of its character (depending on your mood), enter 7334 and read the answer upside down.

$$- \;\; \overset{\displaystyle\square}{\underset{\times}{\overset{=}{\underset{\div}{+}}}} \;\; -$$

Watch the pattern of numbers in the display as you do the following: 11×11, 111×111 and 1111 ×1111. If the calculator had enough display places to let you carry the scheme all the way, you would see the following pleasant symmetry:

1×1	=	1
11×11	=	121
111×111	=	12321
1111×1111	=	1234321
11111×11111	=	123454321
111111×111111	=	12345654321
1111111×1111111	=	1234567654321
11111111×11111111	=	123456787654321
111111111×111111111	=	12345678987654321

$$- \;\; \overset{\displaystyle\square}{\underset{\times}{\overset{=}{\underset{\div}{+}}}} \;\; -$$

Multiply 41096 by 83 and take careful note of the answer—not only the five middle numbers but also the first and last.

$$\begin{array}{c} \Box \\ - \quad = \quad - \\ + \\ \div \\ \times \end{array}$$

Think of a number—any number. Add the digits. Subtract the sum from the original number. The answer will always be an even multiple of 9— that is, it can be divided by 9 with no remainder.

Let's take 752615 as a demonstrator number. Add: $7+5+2+6+1+5=26$; $752615-26=752589$ and $752589 \div 9 = 83621$.

$$\begin{array}{c} \Box \\ - \quad = \quad - \\ + \\ \div \\ \times \end{array}$$

Take a number having any reasonable number of digits (as many as six, say) and go through the following abracadabra:

Multiply by 2.

Add 4.

Multiply by 5.

Add 12.

Multiply by 10.

Subtract 320.

The result will be a number ending in one or more zeroes. Drop them and you will be left with the number that you started with.

Suppose you start with 52871. (You'd better write it down.) Then: $52871 \times 2 + 4 \times 5 + 12 \times 10 - 320 = 5287100$.

$$- \frac{\square}{\substack{= \\ + \\ \div \\ \times}} -$$

Ready for another game of hopscotch? This is an old mathematical trick that the pocket calculator makes easy, although the business does involve some jumping around. You'll probably be able to keep track of things better if you jot down some of the intermediate results. (Losing track of intermediate results is a constant hazard with a pocket calculator. The machine will always give you its output, but it keeps no ready file on the input.)

Okay. Begin with a two-digit number. Call it *a*. Add 6 to it and call the result *b*. Square *a*, clear the calculator and square *b*. Clear again and subtract the smaller of the two squares from the larger one. Call the answer *c*.

Now divide *c* by 12. The result will be a two-digit number. Subtract 3 from it and you will be back to *a*; add 3 to it (the number you got when you divided *c* by 12) and you will be back to *b*.

Suppose you start with 87, which becomes *a*. Adding 6 produces 93, which is *b*. The square of 87 is 7569 and the square of 93 is 8649, so that 8649−7569 gives you 1080 as *c*. Dividing 1080 by 12 yields 90, and 90−3 returns you to 87, while 90+3 gives 93.

We've already had the calculator say hello. It can do the same thing in a breezier way if you multiply 16 by 650.875 and turn the display 180 degrees. Unfortunately, it can't say ho hum, although it could give you (for whatever use you might be able to make of it) ho his (51404).

You can do this kind of thing almost indefinitely. Indeed, if you are willing to accept the marginal proposition that the upside-down 2 can be read as a *z*, the 8 as a *b* and the 9 as a *g*, you can dream up a good many more words. Usually when you have a word with a *z*, a *b* or a *g*, it's best to say it aloud before you give the calculator to somebody so he can read the word. That way he's more likely to see it as a word. The entry 8008, for example, gives "boob" both upside down and right side up, but your victim is likely to think you're one unless you prime him beforehand by saying the word.

The all-purpose 9, which has cropped up here before, is useful in what might be called the lost-digit trick. Write down (or ask somebody else to do it) a four-digit number. Call it a. Add the digits and make a note of the total. Call it b. If a is 6182, for example, b is $6+1+8+2$ or 17.

Now discard one of the original four digits. From the three-digit number that remains, subtract b. Call the result c. Add the digits of c and subtract the result from the next higher multiple of 9. The result will be the digit that you discarded from your original four-digit number.

Suppose you discard the 8 from your original number of 6182. That leaves you 612 as your three-digit number. Then $612-b$ (17) is 595, which you designate as c. Adding the digits of that, you get 19, which you subtract from the nearest higher multiple of 9. In this case the nearest higher multiple of 9 is 27, and $27-19$ restores your lost digit.

One hitch: If the digits of c add up to 9 or 18, you are in a bit of trouble when you are working the trick with somebody else, because the discarded digit could be either 0 or 9. You can still look good by saying, "It's either a zero or a nine."

$$
-\ \overset{\square}{\underset{\times}{\underset{\div}{\underset{+}{=}}}}\ -
$$

Let's start again with a four-digit number—say 1975. Separate it into two numbers, 19 and 75. To the first of these add the next higher number (19+ 20=39) and multiply by 5 and then by 10 (39× 5×10=1950).

Your next move is to pick a number between 10 and 99 and add it to the total you just got. Suppose you pick 43; then 1950+43=1993. Add to this the second half of your original number (1993+75), subtract 50 and the number between 10 and 99 and you will wind up with the original number (1933+75−50−43=1975).

$$
-\ \overset{\square}{\underset{\times}{\underset{\div}{\underset{+}{=}}}}\ -
$$

Reach in your pocket and pull out whatever change is there. Count the amount, and with the total as the starting point (used as a whole number, omitting the decimal) do the following things: multiply by 10, add 1, multiply by 2, add 21 and multiply by 5.

The result will be a number ending in 15. Discard the 15 and subtract 1 from what is left. The answer will be the amount of change you started with.

```
      □
  –   =   –
      +
      ÷
      ×
```

Multiply 4649 by 239 and see what you get in the display. Once over lightly?

```
      □
  –   =   –
      +
      ÷
      ×
```

The display will also do interesting things, this time to the right of the decimal point, when you make 11 a constant divider. Try it first into a lesser number, such as 8, and afterward into larger numbers. (If you go into five-figure numbers, the effect diminishes because there are only four places to the right of the decimal point.)

```
      □
  –   =   –
      +
      ÷
      ×
```

Patterns keep turning up. Make 13 a constant divider and divide it first into 1, 3, 4, 9, 10 and 12 and then into 2, 5, 6, 7, 8 and 11, noticing the first result in each series. (Don't go 1, 2, 3 and so on or you won't see the two separate cyclical patterns.)

[41]

$$-\begin{array}{c}\square\\=\\+\\\div\\\times\end{array}-$$

Two years in recent times have read the same right side up and upside down. They were 1881 and 1961. What will the next such year be?

(On the calculator it's sooner than you might think if you think in terms of numbers as they are usually typed, printed or written by hand. In those terms the answer is 6009. But on the calculator 0, 1, 2, 5, 6, 8 and 9 read upside down, so that such years as 2002, 2112 and 2552 would qualify.)

$$-\begin{array}{c}\square\\=\\+\\\div\\\times\end{array}-$$

Do this one in your head before you do it on the calculator: Divide 80 by ½ and add 7. Did your head come up with the same answer as your calculator?

(If you have trouble with this, do 1÷2 first to find the divisor for 80.)

$$-\begin{array}{c}\square\\=\\+\\\div\\\times\end{array}-$$

Mathematics is such a dignified subject, presented in such a sedate way, that it is surprising to come across a number with an exclamation point, such as 5! In fact, there is nothing exclamatory about it; the exclamation point is a symbol called a factorial sign. It means that the number beside it is to be multiplied by all lower whole numbers. For example, 5! (called "factorial 5") is $5 \times 4 \times 3 \times 2 \times 1 = 120$.

What is surprising (exclamation-point surprising) is how rapidly the number builds up after 5! Try a few on your calculator—say 6!, 7!, 8!, 9!, 10! and 11! By 12! your calculator, if it has an eight-place display, will be displaying whatever symbol it uses to show you that there is an overflow beyond the limits of the display.

Picture yourself as an oil sheik in the Middle East with the delightful problem of having money come in so fast that you have to work your imagination overtime finding things to do with the stuff. In one flight of fancy you decide to make Fibonacci deposits in your bank, starting with $1345 (the closest you can come to making your calculator spell "sheik" when read upside down) and then $710 (which is "oil" upside down), thereafter making each deposit the sum of the previous two: $1345, $710, $2055 and so on. How long would it be before you made a deposit exceeding $10000?

The seventh deposit would be $12405.

Slope into the calculator a three-digit number whose digits slope downward—that is, they are in descending order, as in 865. Reverse them and subtract the smaller number from the larger one. Keep doing this with each new result, making sure that you put the digits in descending order, and within a few steps you will arrive at a three-digit number containing (in some order) the digits 4, 5 and 9.

Suppose your number is 865. Then $865-568=297$; $972-279=693$, and $963-369=594$.

Trying the same thing with four-digit numbers, you will find yourself unable to escape bogging down in 6174, which, put in descending order, is 7641, which reversed is 1467, and $7641-1467=6174$.

Think of a number, even a fairly big one, and then go through the following steps: Multiply by

5, add 6, multiply by 4, add 9, multiply by 5, push=. The result will be a number of at least three digits. Throw out the last two digits and subtract 1 from the number that remains. The answer will be the number you started with.

A trick that isn't usually mentioned in the kind of mathematics courses to which most of us are exposed is that the fifth power of a number always ends with the last digit of the original number. For example, $13^1 = 13$; $13^2 = 169$; $13^3 = 2197$; $13^4 = 28561$, and $13^5 = 371293$. Try a few others on your calculator. (A constant feature comes in handy here; the first step is 1 times your number or your number times 1, depending on which way you enter a constant in your machine, and then five rapid strikes at the=key will get you your result.)

Starting with any number (with more than one digit) that catches your fancy, add to it the same number entered backward. Continue doing this, and before long you will have a number that reads the same way backward and forward.

Suppose you start with 1472. Then 1472+2741=
4213, and 4213+3124=7337.


```
      □
   —  =  —
      +
      ÷
      ×
```


Multiply 14593 by 846 (or 846 by 14593) and
see what you have made your calculator do. Now
try 9739369×9.


```
      □
   —  =  —
      +
      ÷
      ×
```


You can give the calculator an extreme case
of the stuck-needle syndrome by making 999 a
constant divider and dividing it into any number
less than 999.


```
      □
   —  =  —
      +
      ÷
      ×
```


Further intriguing patterns appear when you
make 130 a constant divider. To see them clearly
you should write each answer in a column A or a
column B, according to whether the problem
appears here under A or under B:

A	B
$1 \div 130$	$2 \div 130$
$3 \div 130$	$5 \div 130$
$4 \div 130$	$6 \div 130$
$9 \div 130$	$7 \div 130$
$10 \div 130$	$8 \div 130$
$12 \div 130$	$11 \div 130$

$$\begin{matrix} & \square & \\ - & = & - \\ & + & \\ & \div & \\ & \times & \end{matrix}$$

Enter 12345678 and subtract from it 1234567. Now, for a switch on this theme, work the following calculations (the last one is a bit too big to appear correctly on an eight-digit display) and make a mental or written note of the pattern that shows up in the answers:

$$1 \times 8 + 1 =$$
$$12 \times 8 + 2 =$$
$$123 \times 8 + 3 =$$
$$1234 \times 8 + 4 =$$
$$12345 \times 8 + 5 =$$
$$123456 \times 8 + 6 =$$
$$1234567 \times 8 + 7 =$$
$$12345678 \times 8 + 8 =$$
$$123456789 \times 8 + 9 =$$

As you might expect, perceiving the pattern, the answer to the last calculation works out as 987654321.

Ask a friend to think of a three-digit number in which the digits are all the same (such as 444). Tell him that you don't want to know the number but would like to hear the sum of the digits. Multiply that sum by 37 and you will have the original number.

Choose a two-digit number. If the first digit is smaller than the second, multiply the difference between them by 9 and add the result to the original number. If the first digit is larger than the second, multiply the difference between them by 9 and subtract the result from the original number. In either case the number you end up with will be the reverse of the original number.

Any two-digit number added to its reverse (i.e., 27+72) will give a result that is evenly divisible by 11. The stunt also works for a few three-digit numbers and any four-digit number. You can find out about the three-digit numbers (with or without your calculator) by alternately adding and subtracting the digits of the number you get when you add your original number and its reverse. If the answer is 0 or 11, your result is divisible by 11. For example: 327+723=1050; 1−0+5−0=6—not divisible by 11. Another example: 517+715=1232; 1−2+3−2=0—yes.

Of course, you don't have to go to all this trouble when you have a calculator. Just whang the problem out in a single chain of operations: 8359+9538÷11=1627.

$$- \; \frac{\square}{\substack{= \\ + \\ + \\ \times}} \; -$$

Give a friend three dice and your calculator. (The three dice may be the hardest part of the problem, since dice come in pairs. Unless you run a gambling house, you may not have three dice. Use one of a pair to fill in for the third if you have to.)

Ask your collaborator to put the dice side by side (out of your sight) in any order and to write down a six-digit number of which the first three digits are the numbers on the top faces of the dice (seen from left to right) and the last three digits are the numbers on the opposite faces. A typical number might be 342,435. Now tell him to divide

the six-digit number by 37 and the result by 3
($342,435 \div 37 = 9255$, and $9255 \div 3 = 3085$.) He tells
you the final number and gives you back the
calculator.

Starting with the number he gave you, subtract
7 and divide by 9. The result will be a three-digit
number that is the same as the first three-digits of
his six-digit number. In other words, it will tell you
the order in which he put the dice. And, since you
undoubtedly know what's on the opposite face
of each number on a die (1:6, 2:5, 3:4), you can
tell him what his six-digit number was.

If you square a number, add 1 to the result and
multiply the new number by the original one, you
will always end up with an even number.

On the calculator the easy way to work this
with, say, 79 is: $79 \times 79 + 1 \times 79 = 493118$.

Going into reverse again, you will find that when
you pick a number, reverse it and subtract the
smaller from the larger, the result will always be
evenly divisible by 9. Example: $6124 - 4216 = 1908$;
$1908 \div 9 = 212$. Another example: $783 - 387 = 396$;
$396 \div 9 = 44$.

Pick three consecutive numbers. (It's best that they be under 100 or you will overrun the display.) Multiply them. The result will always be divisible by 3. Running $32 \times 33 \times 34$ through the machine gives you 35904, which, divided by 3, yields 11968.

Think up a number that is not evenly divisible by 7. Cube it—that is, multiply it by itself twice $(3 \times 3 \times 3 = 27)$. The number you get is either 1 less or 1 more than a number that is divisible by 7.

Suppose you start with 44. Then $44 \times 44 \times 44 = 85184$. Either 85183 or 85185 is divisible by 7. If you have a calculator with a chain-constant switch and you use the constant feature for cubing, be sure to clear the machine and take it out of constant before you perform the final steps—that is, taking your cube, adding or subtracting 1 and dividing by 7. Otherwise your result may be wildly wrong.

The square of any number is either evenly divisible by 3 or will give you an answer with nothing but 3's to the right of the decimal point.

For example: $26^2 = 676$; $676 \div 3 = 225.33333$.

This is another way of saying that if you were to work the problem by hand, your square would either divide evenly by 3 or would leave a remainder of 1. Again: $26 \times 26 = 676$; $676 \div 3 = 225\frac{1}{3}$.

More lockjaw. Starting with 3 and going up by 3's (3, 6, 9, 12 and so on), multiply each number by 37.

You can give the machine an even more severe case of lockjaw, overflow symbol and all, by multiplying 12345679 by 9 and its multiples up to 81.

If you have really mastered the multiplication table, you know that $7 \times 999 = 6993$. Pulling 6993 or any lesser multiple of 7 out of your head, multiply it by 143. No matter what multiple of 7 you start with, the answer will have a distinct pattern, from $7 \times 143 = 1001$ to $6986 \times 143 = 998998$ and $6993 \times 143 = 999999$.

$$- \frac{\square}{\substack{= \\ + \\ \div \\ \times}} -$$

Now for some unlockjaw. Ascertain the following:

$$11^2$$
$$111^2$$
$$1111^2$$
$$11111^2$$

At this point a calculator with an eight-digit display will record an overflow, but continue:

$$111111^2$$
$$1111111^2$$

You can see the pattern. Without the overflow the numbers would rise and fall all the way, like the notes you would sound practicing scales on the piano.

$$- \frac{\square}{\substack{= \\ + \\ \div \\ \times}} -$$

Another pattern, a bit more subtle, like the design you might find in a tile floor, appears when you do the following calculations:

$$9 \times 6$$
$$99 \times 66$$
$$999 \times 666$$
$$9999 \times 6666$$

□
= −
+
÷
×

The greatest curiosity about 13 is why so many people are skittish of it, even to the extent of skipping it when numbering the floors of buildings. A lesser-known curiosity of 13 appears when you square it, reverse the answer and find the square root of the reversed number. The square of 13 is 169; reversing that yields 961, and the square root of 961 is 31, which is 13 reversed.

□
= −
+
÷
×

Another curious property of 13 is that it will always be the result when you start with any three-digit number (say 753), repeat it to make a six-digit number (753753) and then divide successively by 7, the original three-digit number and 11 $(753753 \div 7 \div 753 \div 11)$.

Now for the unshakable 9. Take any two-digit number, reverse it and subtract one from the other. (It doesn't matter if you subtract the larger one from the smaller one, winding up with a negative number.) The result will always be evenly divisible by 9.

There is also an almost unshakable 99. When you reverse any three-digit number, provided that at least two of the digits are different, and subtract one number from the other, the result will always be evenly divisible by 99. (Again, don't fret over negative numbers. They're harmless.)

The main reason for presenting this operation is that it has an eye-catching look on the page:

$$1+2+1=$$
$$1+2+3+2+1=$$
$$1+2+3+4+3+2+1=$$
$$1+2+3+4+5+4+3+2+1=$$
$$1+2+3+4+5+6+5+4+3+2+1=$$
$$1+2+3+4+5+6+7+6+5+4+3+2+1=$$
$$1+2+3+4+5+6+7+8+7+6+5+4+3+2+1=$$
$$1+2+3+4+5+6+7+8+9+8+7+6+5+4+3+2+1=$$

However, there is more to it than this. Run down the line of results (4, 9, 16 and so on) and note in a parallel line their square roots.

The finished pattern should look like this:

$$1+2+1=\ 4=2$$
$$1+2+3+2+1=\ 9=3$$
$$1+2+3+4+3+2+1=16=4$$
$$1+2+3+4+5+4+3+2+1=25=5$$
$$1+2+3+4+5+6+5+4+3+2+1=36=6$$
$$1+2+3+4+5+6+7+6+5+4+3+2+1=49=7$$
$$1+2+3+4+5+6+7+8+7+6+5+4+3+2+1=64=8$$
$$1+2+3+4+5+6+7+8+9+8+7+6+5+4+3+2+1=81=9$$

```
   □
 – = –
   +
   ÷
   ×
```

In this serve-yourself operation you will be doing some calculations with five numbers that you think up yourself. Call them *a, b, c, d,* and *e*. (Bear in mind the fact that if any of them is whoppingly large, you may overtax the display.)

Pick the numbers. Now go through the following steps: (1) Multiply *a* and *b*. (2) Divide the product by *c*. (3) Multiply the quotient by *d*. (4) Divide the product by *e*. (5) Divide the answer you get by *a*. (6) Add to the quotient *a*. (7) Make a note of the sum.

Now clear the calculator and proceed as follows. Multiply *b* and *d*, note the result and clear the calculator. Multiply *c* and *e*, note the result and clear the calculator. Now divide the first of these results by the second. Subtract the answer from the sum you got at step 7 and you will be back to *a*.

A caution: Since the calculator keeps on spinning out numbers to the right of the decimal point as long as the display space lasts, the operation $(b \times d) \div (c \times e)$ may give you more decimal numbers than you need when you make the final subtraction that returns you to *a*. Discard the decimal numbers you don't need.

```
    □
 _  =  _
    +
    ÷
    ×
```

Before you limber up your calculator on this one, take a wild guess at the result: $1 \div 2 \div 3 \div 4 \div 5 \div 6 \div 7 \div 8 \div 9$. Now run it through the calculator. Ditto with $1 \times 2 \times 3 \times 4 \times 5 \times 6 \times 7 \times 8 \times 9$.

```
    □
 _  =  _
    +
    ÷
    ×
```

As the calculator had the first word in this book, which was hELLO!, so it should have the last. Ask it if this is the end. To get the response, divide 11934 by 51 and hold the display up to a mirror, but bear in mind that some interesting, if more complicated, games follow.

NUTCRACKER
Suite

$$- \begin{array}{c} \square \\ = \\ + \\ \div \\ \times \end{array} -$$

Squares provide a splendid example of how the pocket calculator makes life easier and poses a threat to the pencil industry. Even if your calculator makes you go through four steps to find the square of, say, 752 (Step 1: enter 752; Step 2: push $\times$ key; Step 3: enter 752, Step 4: push = key), you are way ahead of the pencil-and-paper method in terms of time saved and travail avoided. Probably your calculator offers an even easier option requiring only three steps: enter 752, push $\times$ key, push = key. The display will have the desired square up in lights before you can shift your eyes to it, unless you are one of the rare types who can operate a calculator accurately by touch, so that you can watch the display while it does its thing.

Here is a series of numbers to be squared: 5, 6, 25, 76, 376, 625, and 9376.

You have just encountered automorphs, which are numbers that reappear at the ends of their squares. Indeed, you now know all the automorphs there are up to the four-digit level. At the five-digit level 90625 is the only automorph, but its square is too big to show up on a calculator with an eight-digit display.

```
   □
─  =  ─
   +
   ÷
   ×
```

A throw of seven with a pair of dice is thought to be a good thing and is much sought after in certain dice games. The same number can make your calculator cut a few capers. Take 15873 as a constant multiplier (if your calculator has a constant feature, otherwise just do each multiplication separately) and multiply it by 7, 14, 21 and so on, that is, by multiples of 7. Watch the results.

Now make 7 a constant divider and divide it into 1, 2, 3 and so on except for numbers that are even multiples of 7. With 1, the display on an eight-digit calculator will read 0.1428571. Ignore the last digit on this display and the first one after the decimal point on subsequent displays but keep your eye on 142857. You will see that they go into a merry-go-round act. To put it another way, they are cyclical.

This 142857 can give you a few turns on its own. Multiply it by 2, 3, 4, 5 and 6, watching the display carefully. For a final fillip, try 142857×7.

$$\begin{aligned} \square &= \\ + \\ + \\ \times \end{aligned}$$

Starting with any three single digits, as long as they are different from one another, see if you can find a combination besides 6×21 where the product (126 in this case) contains the digits that you multiplied.

It might strike you that this is a search for a needle in a haystack. In fact, however, there is only one combination to be found. (Hint: One of the multipliers is 51. You therefore can limber up your calculator on some trial multiplications of 51 and the digits from 1 through 9 until you find a combination that gives you an answer containing 5, 1 and the number you multiplied 51 by.)

Answer: 3×51 = 153.

You can drive yourself a bit closer to distraction by trying the same thing with four digits. In this case, as with three, you can arrange them in any way (4716, for example, could be 4×716, 47×16, 471×6, 7×416 and so on).

and 35×41 = 1435.
3159, 15×93 = 1395; 21×87 = 1827; 27×81 = 2187, The possible solutions are: 8×473 = 3784; 9×351 =

$$\square$$
$$=$$
$$+$$
$$+$$
$$\times$$

Imagine a set of chips, each of which bears a number from 0 through 9. They are lined up in the following order: 6328907154.

Problem: Without changing the order except by moving digits from end to end (making, for example, 4632890715), find the two groups that can be multiplied to produce the third group. Here again you can put your calculator through a multiplication drill. (Hint: One multiplier has three digits and one has two; the answer has five.)

Answer: 715 × 46 = 32890.

$$\square$$
$$=$$
$$+$$
$$+$$
$$\times$$

Now you have a set of cards, each of which contains one of the numbers from 1 through 9. They are arranged as follows:

7   28   196   34   5

A quick turn with the calculator will demonstrate that 7×28 is 196. The problem is, while moving no more than five cards, to set up two other pairs that can be multiplied to give a common result in the middle. You will probably need

several multiplying turns with the calculator to
get the result.

2 78 156 39 4. Both 2×78 and 4×39 give 156.

$$\Box = -$$
$$+$$
$$\div$$
$$\times$$

It is a pushover, of course, for the calculator
to come up with the square of a number, say, 28.
You just multiply 28×28, or use a shortcut if your
machine provides one.

You can demonstrate to the calculator that there
is a way to calculate one square from the previous
square. To the square that you already have (784
in the case of 28) add the number that is one more
than twice your original number (2×28+1 or 57
in this example). The number you get (841 here)
will be the square of the number that is one higher
than the number you started with (841 is the
square of 29). On the calculator you would do the
following: 28×28=784; clear; 2×28+1=57; 57+
784=841. Checking, 29×29=841.

For numbers ending in 5 you can teach the calculator another trick. Suppose the number to be
squared is 85. Take the first digit (8) and multiply
it by the next whole number (9). Tack on to the
result (72) the number 25. The answer (7225) is
the square of 85.

If you square the numbers 4, 5 and 6 and add the results (16+25+36), you will find that the total (77) is the same as the sum of the squares of 3, 2, and 8 (9+4+64). Same with $5^2+6^2+7^2=9^2+5^2+2^2$. You can mess around with this kind of thing indefinitely.

If you get bored, see what happens when you make pairs of numbers by taking one number from each side of what you started with and then adding their squares. Suppose you started with $4^2+5^2+6^2=3^2+2^2+8^2$. Ignore the exponents and make pairs such as 43, 52 and 68. You will find that $43^2+52^2+68^2=34^2+25^2+86^2$ (each of the second pairs being obtained by reversing the digits of the corresponding first pair). You could just as well use 42, 58 and 63; then $42^2+58^2+63^2=24^2+85^2+36^2$.

More messing around with squares. If you take the sum of two squares (any two) and multiply it by the sum of two other squares, the result will also be the sum of two squares. For example (keeping the numbers simple): $2^2+3^2=4+9=13$; 5^2+

$6^2 = 25 + 36 = 61$. Now: $13 \times 61 = 793$, which is 27^2 $+ 8^2$ or $729 + 64$.

Take a number that is a multiple of 3. Add the cubes of its digits. (You get a cube, such as 3^3, by multiplying the number by itself twice: $3 \times 3 \times 3 = 27$). Do the same thing with the number that results. Keep on doing this, and eventually you will wind up with 153.

Suppose your starting number is 36. The cube of 3 is 27 and the cube of 6 is 216. The sum of 27 and 216 is 243. Now you want to add the cubes of 2, 4 and 3, which will give you 99. Keep going.

You might also want to see what happens when you add the cubes of the digits in 153.

The famous quantity pi (π), which expresses the ratio of a circle's circumference to its diameter, is stated to five decimal places as 3.14159. (In the nineteenth century an Englishman, William Shanks, who was really hooked on pi spent twenty years laboriously calculating it to 707 places. Unfortunately he made a mistake at the 528th place,

and so the remaining 179 were wrong. In recent times computers have calculated pi to thousands of decimal places.)

Anyway, to get back to the simple 3.14159, can you find a fraction that gives the same result to the first five decimals? You will be looking, of course, for a fraction with a denominator that divides into the numerator approximately three times, so you needn't fool around with any fraction that doesn't reduce to approximately 3/1. (Hint: The fraction you want has three figures in both the numerator and the denominator. So on the calculator you want to do some divisions such as $350 \div 150$ until you come up with 3.14159.)

Answer: $355 \div 113 = 3.1415929$.

There is a fraction—a rather large one—that reduces to ½ but has the remarkable property of containing each of the digits from 1 through 9 just once apiece. Can you find the fraction?

(Hint: The denominator lies between 13,400 and 13,500, and the numerator is of course half of the denominator. The way to go at the problem, therefore, is to mess around dividing such numbers as 13,274 and 13,472 by 2, keeping at it until you get four digits in the display that are all different from the five digits you divided 2 into.)

If you get strung out on this kind of thing, there are similar fractions that reduce to ⅓, ¼, ⅕, ⅙, ⅐, ⅛ and ⅑.

In case you verge on collapse over all this, or the calculator does, here are the fractions:

$$\frac{1}{2} = \frac{6729}{13458} \qquad \frac{1}{3} = \frac{5823}{17469} \qquad \frac{1}{4} = \frac{3942}{15768} \qquad \frac{1}{5} = \frac{2769}{13845}$$

$$\frac{1}{6} = \frac{2943}{17658} \qquad \frac{1}{7} = \frac{2394}{16758} \qquad \frac{1}{8} = \frac{3187}{25496} \qquad \frac{1}{9} = \frac{6381}{57429}$$

$$\begin{array}{c} - = \dfrac{\square}{+} = - \\ + \\ \times \end{array}$$

The pocket calculator is slick at calculating square roots—even slicker if it has a square-root key, but that is a fancier calculator than the reader of this book is assumed to have.

Assuming that yours is of the +, −, × and ÷ type, here is a quick, easy and reliable method of working out a square root:

Suppose the number for which you want the square root is 783. Well, 20×20=400 and 30×30= 900, so the square root of 783 must lie between 20 and 30. Let's try 25. Divide 783 by 25; the result is 31.32. Now add your 25 and your 31.32 and divide by 2; the result is 28.16. Make 28.16 your trial square root and go through the whole business again: $783 \div 28.16 = 27.805397$, and $28.16 + 27.805397 \div 2 = 27.982698$. That must be pretty close, so try squaring it. Your answer is 783.03138, which is about as close as you are likely to want to come with the square root of 783.

It doesn't really matter if your first stab is badly off the mark; the method will soon correct it, but it will take more steps.

What if you want the square root of a rather big number, where making that first stab is much tougher than with a number like 783? Here the trick is to break your number up into pairs, starting at the right and working to the left. (If you are working with a decimal number, such as .72175, start at the decimal point and work to the right.) How about the square root of 68,524? Making pairs from the right, you obtain 6   85   24.

Now you want the largest number whose square will fit into the first digit or the first pair. In this case the number is 2, since the square of 2 is 4 and the square of 3 is 9, which won't fit into your first digit, 6. String a zero onto your starting number for each remaining pair, which gives you 200. Making that your trial square root, proceed as follows: $68524 \div 200 + 200 \div 2 = 271.31$. Drop the numbers to the right of the decimal point and repeat the operation with 271, as follows: $68524 \div 271 + 271 \div 2 = 261.92804$. Again dropping the decimal numbers and repeating the operation with 261, you get 261.77203. That must be close, so try squaring it. You get 68524.595, which isn't bad.

Take a still bigger number, such as 521,374. Breaking it into pairs, you get 52 13 74. The biggest number whose square will fit into 52 is 7; adding a zero for each remaining pair, you get 700 as your trial square root. (If you work it through and don't get 722.0623 on the second pass, it's back to the dunce cap for you.)

If you are far enough into mathematics to want to find the square root of a decimal number, the scheme is much the same, except that as we said, you make pairs by starting at the decimal point and working to the right.

Now that you know all that, here's a square-root game. Pick a number. Add 2 to it and then multiply the original number by the larger one. Add 1 to the answer and calculate the square root of the result. Subtract 1 from the answer and you will be back to your original number.

(Fact is, you don't need to go through any elaborate calculation to find the square root. Consider the problem as educational. The square root you want will always be your original number plus 1.)

Suppose your starting number is 21. Then: $21 + 2 = 23$; $21 \times 23 = 483$; $483 + 1 = 484$; $\sqrt{484} = 22$, and $22 - 1 = 21$.

$$- \genfrac{}{}{0pt}{}{\Box}{\begin{matrix} = \\ + \\ \div \\ \times \end{matrix}} -$$

In recreational mathematics, as in stunt flying, there is such a thing as looping. Start with a positive whole number. If it is an even number, divide by 2; if it is odd, multiply by 3 and add 1. Do the same thing with the result and keep going in that way, building up a series. Eventually you will be into a loop that goes 4, 2, 1, 4, 2, 1 . . . .

Suppose you start with 88. That's even, so you divide by 2 and get 44 as the next number in the series. Working the same way you get 22 as the third number in the series and 11 as the fourth. That's odd, so you triple it and add 1 to arrive at 34 as the fifth number. From there on the series proceeds as follows: 34, 17, 52, 26, 13, 40, 20, 10, 5, 16, 8, 4, 2, 1, 4, 2, 1, 4 . . . .

You may find that it takes a long time to get into the loop. A starting number of 27 will put you in that predicament. (It takes 109 steps; along the way you will be as high as 9232—at Step 77—

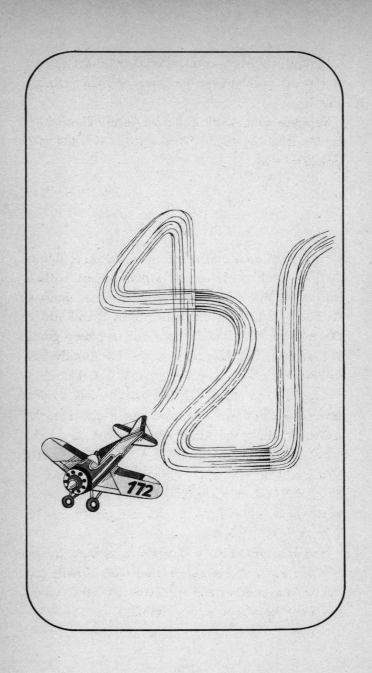

before you start working your way back down to
4, 2, 1, 4 . . . .) On the other hand, if you start with
3, you will be into the loop in five steps.

$$- \frac{\square}{\begin{smallmatrix} = \\ + \\ \div \\ \times \end{smallmatrix}} -$$

The a and b again in this puzzle don't make it
algebra; the letters merely serve to show that you
are working with two different numbers. You could
call them John and Mary.

Make a a number from 3 to 10. Add 5 to it and
call the result b. (Presumably you've done this in
your head. If you've done it on the calculator, you
should now clear the machine.) Now, on the calculator, square a (on any calculator you can
square a number such as 6 by pushing the 6 key,
the $\times$ key, the 6 key again and finally the $=$ key,
and on some you have the easier option of pushing
6, $\times$ and $=$). Note the result, clear the machine
and square b. Add the results of the two squaring
operations and double the answer. Subtract 25 from
what you get. Calculate the square root of the
result. (It won't be a dreadful number like
3.1415926 but a simple number like 13, and you
can arrive at it by squaring a few plausible
numbers until you get the one whose square root
you want.) Subtract 5, divide by 2 and you will
have a. Add 5 and you will have b.

Suppose you choose 6 as a. Then b is 11. The

square of 6 is 36 and the square of 11 is 121; 36+
121×2 is 314. Subtracting 25 gives you 289. To find
the square root of that try squaring, say, 21. Since
that squares to 441, it is too big; try squaring 17
and you will have the number you want. From 17
subtract 5 and divide by 2 and you are back to
6; add 5 and you are back to 11.

Your calculator will take you part way down a
road that has attracted specialists in the theory of
numbers for many centuries. In general terms the
assertion is that $x^p - x$ will be evenly divisible by p
if p is a prime number. (The first five primes,
which are defined as numbers that are divisible
only by themselves and 1, are 1, 2, 3, 5 and 7.)

For example, $2^5 - 2 = 30$, which is evenly divisible by 5; $3^5 - 3 = 240$, ditto. The rule is good for
any x and any p. Your calculator will demonstrate
the principle up to 10^7, after which it will run out
of display space if it has an eight-place display.

You have an alternative, though, of keeping x
small and going on to higher primes: 11, 13, 17, 19
and 23 will carry you about to the limit. Try it
with 2^{23}.

The calculator is prepared to tell you that you have now really come to the end. Find the square root of 5475600 and hold the display up to a mirror.

About the Author

JAMES T. ROGERS is a member of the board of editors of *Scientific American*. Following his graduation from Harvard College in 1942 he spent three years as a field artillery officer in the U.S. Army and then began work as a newspaper reporter in Binghamton, New York, the city in which he was born and grew up. From 1951 to 1955 he was a reporter in the Washington bureau of the Gannett Newspapers. He then spent a year as press secretary to U.S. Senator Irving M. Ives and six years as a writer of the Review of the Week at *The New York Times* before joining *Scientific American* in 1963. In his spare time he reads a lot, plays as much tennis as he can, takes care of two old houses and the land around them, and keeps a hive of bees.